Jeremy Cohen's
Make Your Fiddle Swing!
Solos and Duets for Violin

- Melodies and chord progressions for 15 jazz classics plus 19 solos and 10 duets for intermediate players of all styles

- Practical tips for improving your playing technique and making your fiddle swing!

- Play along with Jeremy and a real band!

- Stream audio and play along at both slow and regular tempos

- Play in duet with Jeremy

- Explore ideas for expressing swinging rhythms with your bow arm

- Tips on improvising and playing swing and jazz

Violinjazz Publishing
Oakland, California

© 2018 Violinjazz Publishing (ASCAP)

ISBN: 9780984471188

All rights reserved. No part of this publication may be reproduced in any form or by any means without the prior written permission of the publisher.

Published by Violinjazz Publishing

3542 Fruitvale Ave. #147, Oakland, CA 94602 • (877) 678-5299

www.violinjazzpublishing.com

Printed in the U.S.A.

21st Century Blues, *Clouds and Shadows*, and *Django's Djazz Blues* composed by Dix Bruce (BMI)

Jeremy's Jamboree composed by Jeremy Cohen (ASCAP)

All other songs are in the public domain.

Arrangements and texts by Jeremy Cohen

Music preparation by Robert Puff, RPM Seattle

Photography (except where noted) and book design by Dix Bruce

Audio tracks recorded by Dix Bruce

Audio tracks performers:
- Jeremy Cohen, violin
- Dix Bruce, guitar
- Jason Vanderford, guitar
- Marty Eggers, string bass

Jeremy Cohen

Photo by Hasain Rasheed

Table of Contents

Getting Started 7

    Audio Tracks 8

    Playing with the Audio Tracks 8

    Practicing for Tempo 9

    Important Terms and Tips 10

    Symbols: Articulation, Dynamics, and Tempo 11

    What makes music swing? 12

Right (Bow) Arm 13

    Definitions 13

    Tips for relaxing your bow arm 13

    Tips for your right hand bow grip 14

Left Hand and Arm 16

    Finger pressure 16

    Intonation 16

    Left thumb position 16

    Left elbow position 18

Topic Sidebars

    About the Author 19

    Bow Use in Tripletted Swing Rhythms 20

    What Is Improvisation? 36

    Economy of Motion 41

    Are you holding your instrument with tension? 65

    Interpretation: Moving from Classical to Jazz 69

    Vibrato 84

    Rhythmization 90

Music (with Tutorials, Melodies, Improvisations, and Duets)

    21st Century Blues – *Craft an improvisation* 20

    Limehouse Blues

        Interpretation of melody, Retake of the bow 26

    St. James Infirmary – *Tripletted swing bowing* 32

    Clouds and Shadows – *Creating a lyrical line* 36

    Whispering – *Positioning the fingers for accurate intonation* 39

    El Choclo – *Rhythmic solidarity* 45

    Indiana – *Right arm and bow coordination* 51

    Django's Djazz Blues – *Transpositions and hooked bowings* 58

    Red Wing Swing

        Bow use for long and short notes

        Understanding the balance point and weight of the bow 62

    Stumbling – *Springy energy in the right hand and arm* 68

    Tiger Rag – *Light and active bow arm and wrist* 73

    Jeremy's Jamboree – *Developing your own solos* 80

    Have Pity – *Smooth legato playing and long bow strokes* 83

    I Ain't Got Nobody – *Rhythmizing the melody* 87

    Way Down Yonder in New Orleans – *Expressing solid time* 92

Wrapping Things Up 96

More by Jeremy Cohen 98

Quartet San Francisco, Fall 2018

Photo by Hasain Rasheed

Getting Started

Greetings, and welcome to Jeremy Cohen's *Make Your Fiddle Swing!*

This book explores practical concepts for developing rhythm and improvisation skills. And while we're at it, we'll also cover some violin mechanics in order to loosen up and play with more fluidity. The rhythm and improvisation concepts built into these solos and duets were designed by a string player *for* string players. Players of other instruments can also learn from many of the subjects addressed here. If you are one of those non-string players, welcome to our world!

Jazz method books are in abundance, but few address the concepts and techniques related specifically to string players. We have our own set of issues relating to improvisation. Take comfort in knowing that a fellow string player understands right where you are. This book is designed to take you to the next level.

In my teaching studio I encourage students to make the simplest connection between where they are and where they'd like to be. This seems easier to me than suffering over a problem or a new technical challenge. So check your doubts and fears at the door, and let's adopt a process that pursues our best image of ourselves, doing the thing we love the most—fearlessly playing music and having a great time doing it.

As players of bowed instruments, many of us have had training that focuses our studies on music printed on a page; therefore, the path to improvisation can feel like a daunting journey. But when improvisation is explained to us by a fellow string player it can make much more sense, and we can then begin to see positive changes in our own playing. Recognizing small improvements can be very exciting, but real progress takes patience, a healthy dose of concentration, and willingness to evaluate (and listen to) our own playing.

> Unless your plan is to stay put in front of your computer screen and play solo, you will likely feel a yearning to get out and play with other musicians. And once you do that, I guarantee you'll collect plenty of new musical cohorts along the way.

Remember, our goal as musicians is joy and self-expression. Your job is to connect as purely as possible with your musical voice, and express it as cleanly as you can through your instrument. With this goal in mind, focus on the many tips inside these pages for improving your tone, intonation, and playing posture while learning these pieces.

Audio Tracks

Each of the fifteen pieces in the book comes with a set of audio tracks: you'll find them on the Violinjazz Publishing website at **violinjazzpublishing.com/violin-swing-1**.

If you'd like to keep the audio tracks handy on a CD, just follow the purchase link on the web page to order one. Note that the website menus will not guide you to the audio tracks page, so you'll want to bookmark the page **violinjazzpublishing.com/violin-swing-1** for easy access! The tracks are available for your use with the purchase of the book. They are not downloadable.

Playing with the Audio Tracks

The recordings present the first violin in the left channel and the second violin in the right channel. You can isolate either part by using a single headphone, earbud, or speaker. The backup band is audible in both channels. Adjust the balance control on your playback device to hear more or less of one or the other part. If you are listening on headphones and don't have a balance control, simply take one earpiece off to simulate the balance control.

The regular speed versions of the solos are recorded at moderate tempos. Out in the real world, and without this book, these pieces can be played at whatever speed you choose. Always keep in mind that speed is only one of many aspects of playing well. Most folks would rather hear something slow and clean, as opposed to fast and messy, so try not to concern yourself too much with tempo.

Be careful to tailor your improvisations to match rhythmically with the ending sequence performed by the band. In some cases the rhythm may be altered to signal the end is coming, or some bars will be repeated to create an ending sequence. I'm leaving it to you to decide how you will play these endings.

Practicing for Tempo

Metronomes can be very helpful in getting a solo up to speed. Here's what I do: I start practicing a solo with the metronome set at a comfortable speed. Next I decide what my up-to-speed goal is, then I work toward it in increments of three to five clicks on the metronome. Keep track of your progress in a bound music notebook or electronic device. That way you'll have all your work and notes together in one place. (I have learned that notebooks are more difficult to lose or misplace than a single sheet of paper.)

Metronomes are available in a huge variety of sizes, prices, and packages. You can still find the old-fashioned mechanical models, but electronic, battery-operated models are much smaller, more economical, and come with more features than traditional metronomes. Of course, if you enjoy life on the cutting edge, you can use a metronome that's available on the Internet or download one for your smartphone or tablet. Several are available free of charge.

If you want to go the extra distance and work on tempo at your own pace, contact info@musixnow.com to purchase the audio CD and use it in combination with an app that lets you slow down or speed up audio files in very small increments. I've had great luck with an app called Amazing Slow Downer (ronimusic.com), though there are several similar programs and apps on the market.

No matter what additional aids you use, work toward a consistent tempo. Identify the most difficult spot in the piece, and play from the beginning at the speed where you can perform that most difficult part. It won't help if you breeze through the easy parts and then readjust the tempo when you get to the hard parts.

Important Terms and Tips

Articulation: Articulation refers to the manner in which a note is played, i.e. long or short, detached or connected.

Audio tracks spoken introductions: The spoken introductions on the audio tracks coincide with the titles and subtitles on the printed pages.

Audio tracks violin and band parts: The first violin part will always be on the left channel (or side), while the second violin part will always be on the right. The backup band will be heard equally on both sides. If you have the capability to isolate the violin tracks by panning to the right or left, you can isolate the first or second violin part and play along with either track as a solo or duet.

Duet: The word comes from the Latin duo, which means two. Two musicians playing together are called a duet, and the music they play together is also called a duet. The same is true for a trio, quartet, and quintet—these terms refer to the players collectively, but it can also mean the music they play, as in, "Come on over and play some trios with us."

Dynamics: Loud (f or forte) and soft (p or piano), as well as many other terms and symbols, are referred to as dynamics. They tell us to play loud, soft, or in between.

Improvisation: My improvised interpretations of the songs are based on their specific melodies and chordal structures.

Improvisation and duet: Some improvisations are paired with a second line which harmonizes (or plays in duet with) the top line.

Melody: A song's melody is the singable tune that defines the composition. It will appear as a single line or, in most cases, as the top line of a two-line score.

Melody and duet: A melody and duet are written on two staves of music, showing the melody line on the top and the harmonized line (which can be higher or lower in range) on the bottom. The two lines are intended to be played simultaneously as a duet. In most cases the second line can also be played as an alternative solo or single line.

Play-along band tracks: The play-along band tracks are for use with the corresponding printed pages, or to accompany any improvising you may want to do on your own. You'll find instructions for accessing the tracks in "Audio Tracks."

Symbols: Articulation, Dynamics, and Tempo

	Definitions	
>	Accent	Play the note with an articulated beginning point
(arpeggio notation)	Arpeggio	The notes of a chord played in succession (ascending or descending)
<	Crescendo	Increasing volume or intensity expressed over a series of notes
>	Decrescendo (or diminuendo)	Diminishing volume or intensity expressed over a series of notes
•	Dot (staccato)	Short note with a stop after note is played
—	Dash (tenuto)	Hold the note for the full duration of its printed value
rit.	Ritard or ritardando	Slow down ("relax") the tempo
⌢	Slur	A curved line above or below a series of notes indicating that they are to be bowed together in the same bow direction and played smoothly
⌢	Tie	Curved line between two successive notes of the same pitch whose value is combined into one single note

Jeremy Cohen's **Make Your Fiddle Swing!**

What makes music swing?

Swing is a rhythmic language. Similar to spoken language, it can take many shapes. Think about the many dialects that occur in different regions of your own country. Do people sound different from north to south, east to west? Do they have accents? Yes! The same concept is true in jazz.

> Experimentation on our instruments can lead us to better ideas. If you try new ways of doing things and allow yourself to make mistakes, you will eventually discover a unique voice informed by your imagination. That's the voice we are seeking!

Part of training yourself to play in a new genre is to learn the choreography. Essential to creating swing is how we rhythmize our playing so that it speaks in a "jazzy" way. In a sense, we are teaching our right arm and body to feel swinging rhythm, bringing a jazzy style into our performance. Much of this has to do with using the bow arm to create articulations, which notes we choose to play long or short. Try to follow the bowings exactly. Play the dotted notes short and the dashed notes long, but in most cases, leave the bow on the string and don't pick it up unless it's necessary to do so.

The many articulation marks (dots and dashes) will help you understand, and in some cases replicate, how my playing achieves its rhythmic voice. Remember, different players will choose different accents. My efforts here are to share my playing style with you in order to help you develop your own rhythmic voice.

Right (Bow) Arm

Definitions	
Frog	Block of carved wood at the base of the bow attached to the stick with an adjustable tension screw
Tip	Point of bow with a carved box for one end of the bow hair
Middle point	Middle point of the bow hair
Balance point	The point at which the weight of the bow is evenly distributed (fig. 13)
Upper half (UH)	Middle point of hair to bow tip
Lower half (LH)	Middle point of hair to frog
Down bow and up Bow	Directions of bow travel, either from the frog toward the tip, or the tip toward the frog

Tips for relaxing your bow arm

Allow yourself to feel the natural organic weight of your right arm suspended from your shoulder. Invite the feeling of gravity upon and through that arm. Use just enough energy to keep the arm suspended above the floor, rather than feeling as though your energy is dropping down from the ceiling.

It's important to know just how little energy it takes to play the violin effectively—too many players frequently force too much intensity and muscle strength into their instruments through the right arm. Do take some time to experiment with degrees of weight your bow arm puts upon the string. Also spend time experimenting with the relationship between speed and pressure, which has a direct impact on your tone production and volume as well. You will improve your control over your sound production more than you realize is even possible, and it's fun to spend some quality time discovering the nuances of your sound production.

Avoid pushing or forcing the bow into the string with the weight of the arm. Rather than using pressure from your bow-hand fingers, let gravity and the weight of the bow allow it to float on the surface of the string. Most bows weigh only two ounces (see page 58), which is plenty of gravitational weight to make a solid tone, so you won't need to press into the string to produce more sound. The result will offer you and the listener a relaxed sound as opposed to one fueled by tension.

If you do want more volume, try adding more horizontal motion or speed to your bow stroke. Then match that with the slightest possible additional pressure towards the string from the right hand fingers. There is a lot to discover here, and I encourage you to experiment with varying rates of speed and pressure, and listen to the resulting variations in tone.

Tips for your right hand bow grip

This series of photographs offers a good look at the way I hold the bow. These pictures were shot from multiple angles to show a few different aspects of my bow grip.

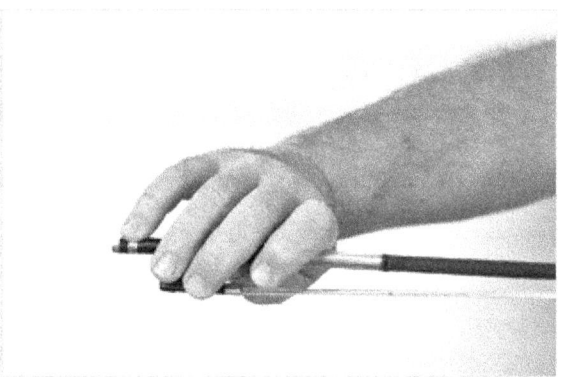

Fig. 1. Bow hold, top view. The fingers are curved and relaxed over the stick. Look for the following:

- A small gap between the index finger and second finger
- Second and third fingers together, over the frog between the first and second knuckle
- A small gap for the little finger, which rests on top of the stick and serves as a counterweight, poised to gradually absorb the bow's natural weight as the it approaches the frog on an upbow stroke.

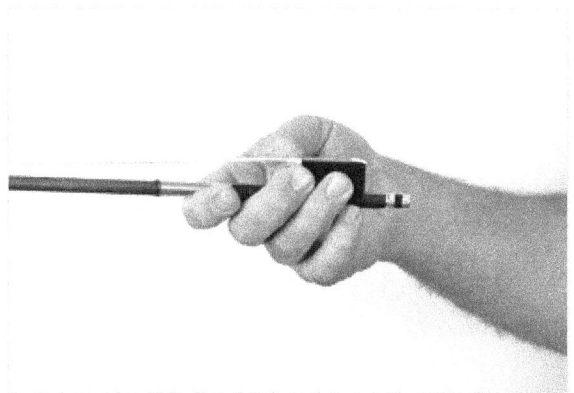

Fig. 2. Bow hold, view of bottom of hand. My thumb supports the stick from below with a natural bend or curve. It is not flexed against the stick.

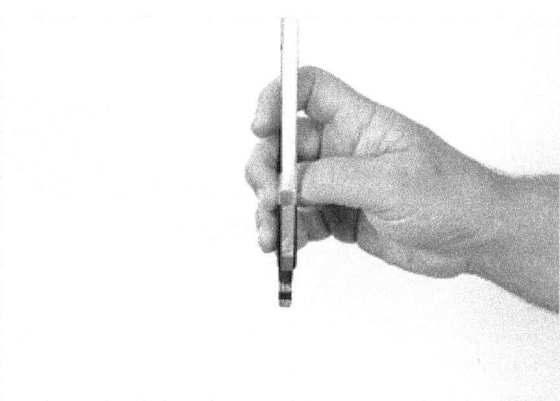

Fig. 3. Bow hold, upright view. You can see the inside of my hand, with my fingers wrapped around the top of the stick, and my thumb rounded (without squeezing the bow).

Fig. 4. Bow hold, view of curve. My thumb supports the stick from below with a natural bend or curve rather than flexing against the stick.

Left Hand and Arm

Finger pressure

How much pressure does it really take to produce a sound without sounding fuzzy, and how does that compare with the amount of pressure you normally use? Do you find yourself grappling with how to move more quickly around the fingerboard? It probably won't surprise you to learn that finger pressure and bow speed are related.

If you want to increase the speed of your left hand fingers, consider using less downward pressure onto the fingerboard. Test out this concept by using not quite enough left hand finger pressure to produce a solid tone. Now, very slowly add finger pressure until you hear a solid tone. Then stop adding pressure. Assess this level of finger pressure as compared to the finger pressure level you're accustomed to. Is it lighter? For most of us the answer will be yes. In my opinion most players use far more finger pressure than is actually necessary to produce an acceptable tone. Your finger speed and agility will also increase by using just enough pressure to deliver a solid tone. Using more pressure than is necessary will only slow you down.

Intonation

Practice anticipating distances between your left hand fingers before you execute a note. Know in advance what a half step and a whole step feels like. Consciously train a working relationship between your inner ear, brain, and fingers to deliver accurate intonation. If you miss a note, don't wiggle it into the right place. Pick up your finger and replace it with better accuracy. The more you practice accurately hearing the pitch inside your ear before you play it, the more accurate your intonation will be. This process of hearing music internally (separate from sounds actually being heard through our ears) is called audiation, and experienced players are audiating all the time.

Left thumb position

Our left thumb position is both a technical issue and a matter of personal preference, and it can differ from player to player. Take a look at the photos below of my left hand position, shown from the side and as I'm looking over my shoulder. My thumb is across from and slightly behind my first finger (fig. 5). Yours may differ, depending on what you find comfortable.

Make sure you don't squeeze the neck of the instrument with your thumb—that will only slow down your fingers. The thumb and crook of the hand provide a counter balance or gentle cushion for the downward pressure of the fingers (fig. 6). Your thumb also serves as a guide for shifting up and down the neck of the instrument without squeezing or clenching. Make sure everything here in the left hand remains pliable. Unnecessary tension causes issues with tone production and intonation and it hinders speed and accuracy.

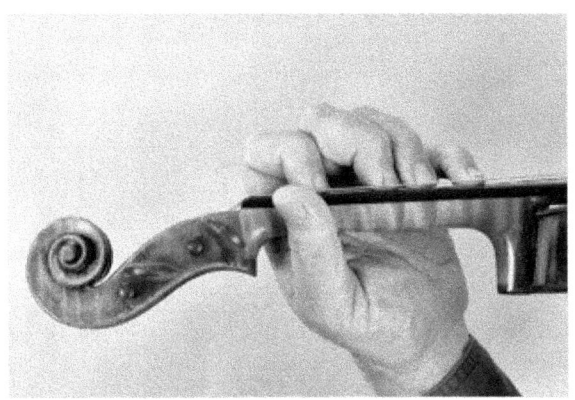

Fig. 5. Thumb and first finger position

Fig. 6. The thumb and crook of the hand

Left elbow position

Your left elbow should be able to rotate freely from your shoulder and hover loosely beneath the instrument (fig. 7). A simple pivot of your shoulder and elbow will allow the fingertips to approach each string at a consistent angle (fig. 8). Stay relaxed in your shoulder to maintain that consistent angle—it helps intonation and keeps the fingers in close proximity to the string you need to play on (fig. 9). In summary, shoulder is relaxed, feel the natural weight of your arm, and your elbow should be hanging freely from your shoulder (fig. 10).

Fig. 7. Left elbow hovers beneath the instrument

Fig. 8. Shoulder and elbow pivot

Fig. 9. Maintain a dropped, relaxed shoulder

Fig. 10. Elbow and shoulder rotating freely

One more thing before we get to the music and recordings. That's me, Jeremy Cohen, on the violin, Dix Bruce on guitar, Jason Vanderford on guitar, and Marty Eggers on string bass. We hope you enjoy playing along with us and that you'll make it a part of your daily practice routine. We'll never get tired and will be right there backing you up as you practice a melody, an improvisation, or your own solos and inventions.

Now, let's get swinging!

Jeremy Cohen

About the Author

Active as both a jazz and classical violinist, Jeremy Cohen has served on the faculties of the Stanford Jazz Workshop in Palo Alto, the Jazzschool in Berkeley, and the Henry Mancini Institute in Los Angeles. He tours with his two bands and is an active studio musician.

Jeremy has extensive experience playing jazz, tango, classical, bluegrass, country, blues, rock, and funk. He founded the Violinjazz Quartet in 1986 (piano, guitar, bass, and violin), and Quartet San Francisco (string quartet) in 2001. He composes, arranges, and publishes most of the quartet's unique literature.

In recent decades, Jeremy has performed throughout the world giving concerts in China, Argentina, Turkey, Japan, South Korea, New Caledonia, Italy, Germany, England, and Scotland. He has performed live on stage with artists such as Frank Sinatra, Tony Bennett, Sammy Davis Jr., Dizzy Gillespie, Johnny Mathis, Gladys Night, Smokey Robinson, Natalie Cole, and George Benson.

He has worked in Broadway shows and on television series, movie soundtracks, and video game scores. Over the years he has recorded with artists such as Carlos Santana, Linda Ronstadt, Aaron Neville, Kitaro, John Williams, Dame Cleo Laine, Ray Charles, Tower of Power, Turtle Island Quartet, and many more. In addition to composing and arranging, he appears as a solo jazz and tango violinist with symphony orchestras.

Jeremy's own CDs have received seven Grammy nominations. His most recent recordings are "The Music of Eddie South" (Sono Luminus) with Violinjazz and "A QSF Journey" (Reference Recordings) with Quartet San Francisco.

Jeremy's broad experience and understanding of genres beyond classical music uniquely qualify him to guide inquisitive string players in expanding their playing opportunities and learning to navigate the many arenas of contemporary music.

21st Century Blues

Craft an improvisation by referencing the melody

When playing improvisations, I like to identify which components of the melody seem interesting to me. I do that by figuring out a recognizable "musical snapshot," which uses motifs from the song's melody. This helps to differentiate one improvisation from another, making it unique and crafted to that specific song.

Take a look at the first few bars of the melody—a few of these bars begin with a rhythmic pattern of two or three quarter notes. I noticed this element and used it as a jumping-off point in my improvisation.

The improvisation starts with a sustained B-flat (5 beats) and then references the beginning of the melody in Bar 2, quoting the melody but with a twist. This idea lets the listener know that I am responding to the melody of this specific song by referencing it in my improvisation.

Here's another example: look in the melody at Bar 7. I use this same bit in Bar 7 of the improvisation. I think you get the idea here that I'm not just freely improvising, I'm using or quoting components of the melody to craft my improvisation.

Some players have a tendency to base their solos purely on the chords they are playing. While learning to understand the chordal structure of a song is vital, I also want to keep the song's melody in mind while improvising. That way I'm drawing my improvisations from both the melody and the chordal structure of the song simultaneously.

Here are some similarities between the melody and the improvisation.

- The chromatic movement in the second half of Bar 6 (melody) is mimicked in the chromatic movement in Bars 2 and 7 of the improvisation.

- The rhythm in Bar 8 of the melody is mirrored in Bars 8 and 24 of the improvisation.

- The octave leap in Bar 7 of the melody (a favorite of mine!) is reflected in the corresponding bar of the improvisation.

In the melody and duet notice the subtle "fall offs" I am playing in bars 14 and 15 in both parts. These are style components which I occasionally add when playing in a swing genre. I am gently releasing my finger at the end of the note and letting the finger trail down the fingerboard while still applying an extremely light touch to the bow to keep the sound going, giving a very gentle "meow" type effect to the tail of the note. I am simulating the sound of a saxophone or trombone to give added emphasis to the swing or Dixieland feel of this song.

I point these out in order to help you understand how improvising decisions are made by using material taken directly from the song you are playing. You will not only please your playing partners and listeners, but you will also have fun doing it! Give it a try—pick a musical motif, and play around with it in your practice. Don't be afraid of mistakes; use them to guide you to a more successful end result.

In closing, I'll add this note about the duet: I harmonized the second line higher in pitch than the first line. This can be played by either player. For this duet I chose to keep the higher voice in the second part, as a supportive harmonization to the main first-line voice. Check it out. I think you will like the result.

Jeremy Cohen's violin, made in 1868 by Jean Baptiste Vuillaume

Photo by Richard Grant

Jeremy Cohen's Violinjazz at Yoshi's in Oakland, 2010. From left, Larry Dunlap (piano), Cohen, Jim Kerwin (string bass), and Dix Bruce (guitar)

Photo by Bryan Caldwell

21st Century Blues
Melody and Duet

Dix Bruce
arr. Cohen

Copyright © 2018 Violinjazz Publishing (ASCAP) and Dix Bruce Music (BMI)
All rights reserved.
www.violinjazz.com

21st Century Blues
Improvisation

Dix Bruce
arr. Cohen

Copyright © 2018 Violinjazz Publishing (ASCAP) and Dix Bruce Music (BMI)
All rights reserved.
www.violinjazz.com

21st Century Blues Improvisation page 2

Limehouse Blues
Interpretation of melody
Retake of the bow

In notating this piece, I decided to leave the whole notes in place in Bars 4, 8, and 12 (instead of changing them to half notes, or dotted half notes with rests) to allow you to determine for yourself when to pick up the bow and return to the frog to restart the melody in the following bar. Here is the reason why: jazz charts are typically notated without consideration for bowings (or breath marks, for vocalists). It's up to us to figure out where we need to adjust our playing to suit the needs of the piece being played.

Let's analyze this so you can see why. If you leave your bow on the string for the full value of the whole notes in Bars 4, 8 and 12, you will find yourself at the tip of the bow, and you'll need to continue the melody from an *up bow*. Maintaining the intensity of the melodic line from there will be a challenge—keeping up that melodic forward push is much more easily done from the middle or lower half of the bow. Therefore, picking up the bow in this moment and placing it closer to the middle (or frog) is a good move. You'll also need to shorten the length of the whole notes in Bars 4, 8, and 12, as well as Bars 20, 24, and 28.

Now you've seen a good example of a string player's moment of decision making. You've arrived at something on the page that requires your revision—you decide to stop the bow after three beats of the whole note (or wherever it sounds best) to give yourself time to retake the bow back to the frog, or lower half of the bow. From this new bow location you can continue the song with a more confident and secure tone.

Notice the dashes in Bars 25, 26, 27, and 31 in Improvisation #1. Listen to how I play them in the audio track—I put a bit of stress and length on them in order to mark the downbeats and strengthen the rhythm in those bars. It's a stylistic decision to bring some rhythmic punctuation to the arpeggiated line there. Try it yourself. It gives the rhythm equal importance to the melody, which is an important concept in developing a swing style.

Look for the additional half note and quarter note backup parts for Limehouse Blues. I added these because when you play this with other players, you'll need to play something that helps keep the rhythm going and expresses the chords at the same time. Look at them carefully and see how each double stop is a part of the chord structure. You can practice these patterns and use them to replicate a rhythm instrument. Joining the band and playing a supportive role for other soloists is a great idea!

Limehouse Blues
Melody

Philip Braham & Douglas Furber
arr. Cohen

Copyright © 2018 Violinjazz Publishing (ASCAP)
All rights reserved.
www.violinjazz.com

Limehouse Blues
Improvisation N° 1

Braham and Furber
arr. Cohen

Limehouse Blues
Improvisation Nº 2

Braham and Furber
arr. Cohen

Limehouse Blues
Half Note Backup

Braham and Furber
arr. Cohen

* double stops throughout

Limehouse Blues
Quarter Note Backup

Braham and Furber
arr. Cohen

* double stops throughout

St. James Infirmary
Tripletted swing bowing

Each song has its unique thumbprint, and this one is an A-minor blues tune with a slow and swaying to-and-fro groove. Let's have a closer look at how we can apply some creative thinking and musical ideas to get the music swaying.

St. James Infirmary carries a strong 12/8 feel: the four quarter-note beats each carry a triplet division. Be aware of this underlying rhythm and feel the subdivisions as you play this piece.

One-and-a *two*-and-a *three*-and-a *four*-and-a,
OR
Ham-bur-ger *ham*-bur-ger *ham*-bur-ger *ham*-bur-ger,
OR (if you are a vegetarian),
Broc-co-li *broc*-co-li *broc*-co-li *broc*-co-li.

Notice that the accents in the above phrases are on the first syllable, the first of each group of three eighth notes.

I wrote the first verse intentionally as pairs of eighth notes. Grouped in twos, we can read this rhythm of two eighth notes in two different ways—as straight eighth notes (equal in length and emphasis, more typical in classical music), or as eighth notes with a tripletted feeling to them. Long-short Long-short, or dash-dot dash-dot. For playing in the swing idiom, we generally choose the jazzy tripletted 12/8 feel. Even though you see dashes on both notes of beat 2 of Bars 1 and 3, the first note will last longer than the second note. This long-short pattern is typical in the swing jazz idiom. You'll give two-thirds of the time to the long note and the remaining third to the short note, while leaving the bow down on the surface of the string.

Notating the eighth notes to look equal is typical in jazz charts, and it frequently has to do with the amount of space required on the page: a piece written in triplets requires 30 percent more space then when the music is written in eighth notes. The eighth notes you see in Bars 1 through 8 can be played in a long-short bowing pattern, or they could have been spelled out in triplets (as in Bar 9 to the end). They would look very different but would be played a similar way. Sometimes the music gives us all three notes of the triplet (see Bar 9, beat 2). When all three notes are written out, play three equal eighth notes so they combine to equal the time value of a single quarter note.

Notice the comma after the third beat in Bar 16 in the improvisation. This is where the chord sequence ends and a new one begins, so I put the comma there. It's signaling you to put a little breath or space in the music, just as you would when you when you see a comma in a written sentence.

Listen for subtle slides into and out of notes in my performance on the audio tracks. For example, into the down beat of the first full bar, a slight slide into the A gives a bit of bluesy swing feel here. Also the G in the middle of the third full bar has a slide into it. These again are stylistic moves that add a unique type of flavor or accent, adding authenticity to the music. I probably wouldn't do this in a classical piece because it wouldn't be appropriate to the genre, but I think it works great here.

Notice how the backup track slows down at the end. Make sure to slow down with the band so you come in for a smooth landing at the end of the song. This slowing down is called a *ritard* or *ritardando* and is often found at the end of songs.

Bow use in tripletted swing rhythms

The distance of the down bow, which covers the first two notes of the triplet, must be recovered by a slightly more energetic up bow in order to return the bow to its starting place. Otherwise you will find yourself drifting and playing at the tip of the bow, having no idea of how you got there. Has this ever happened to you?

St. James Infirmary
Melody and Rhythmized Melody

Traditional
arr. Cohen

St. James Infirmary
Improvisation

Traditional
arr. Cohen

Clouds and Shadows
Creating a lyrical line

In my improvisation of *Clouds and Shadows* I'd like to accentuate the central motif in the melody. As you can see from the title, this song conjures up clouds and shadows. How can we translate this idea into our playing? Let's discuss.

Notice the triplets throughout the piece, which ascend in a repeated pattern of B-flat to B-natural, followed by a gently descending motif. It's a pattern, so it's repetitive. But when it's all put together within the piece, the result is a comforting rocking motion, both lazy and smooth, and it makes for good listening. When you're playing this pattern think of a swaying motion by imagining yourself in a hammock or a rocking chair, looking up at the clouds. We want to relay this feeling to our audience, so think about how that might be done using your instrument and a bow.

Each time you play the triplet figure, make sure to draw out those eighth notes. Think of them as long and broad, not short. Create a relaxed sound by keeping your bow arm—starting from your shoulder, and down through the elbow, wrist, and fingers—nice and loose. The bowings in this piece give us long smooth lines and keep our bow arm in almost constant, flowing motion.

Look for the comma after beat one in Bar 16 in the improvisation. Its purpose is to mark the break between the first and second phrases. Reflect that in your performance by adding a slight space, a little hesitation, as if you were a singer taking an unhurried breath.

Discovering what does and does not work informs the path to success. It's important to know that, so be willing to try and try again to find what works best for you.

What Is Improvisation?

Think about the distance between two points. In musical improvisation, it's mostly about creatively moving from one chord to another. One important thing to realize is that most jazz and swing players know not only the melodies of the songs they play but also the chord structures.

The more familiar you are with the underlying harmonies of a song, the more you can anticipate the changes coming up before you play over them, and your improvisation will benefit from the homework you've done. This is a useful way of developing your craft.

Clouds and Shadows
Melody

Dix Bruce
arr. Cohen

Copyright © 2018 Violinjazz Publishing (ASCAP) and Dix Bruce Music (BMI)
All rights reserved.
www.violinjazz.com

Clouds and Shadows
Improvisation

Dix Bruce
arr. Cohen

Copyright © 2018 Violinjazz Publishing (ASCAP) and Dix Bruce Music (BMI)
All rights reserved.
www.violinjazz.com

Whispering
Positioning the fingers for accurate intonation

Whispering opens with a verse in a short articulated style, so be sure to observe the dots. When it transitions into a very smooth legato melody in Bar 17, leave the bow down on the string to make a broad legato sound to the end.

Left-hand finger position and economy of motion are concepts that apply to all violin playing across all musical styles. Position the tips of your fingers directly over the string (or strings, when playing double stops) so they have an arched shape.

Fig. 11. Fingers above the A string

My elbow is rotated to allow my fingers to naturally arch between the palm of my hand and the neck of the instrument (fig. 11). My fingertips are directly above the A string, in proper position without any unusual stress. The location of my left elbow accommodates this efficient finger position.

Fig. 12. Position of my left arm and elbow for playing on the G string

I have rotated my elbow from my shoulder to allow my fingers to make an arch between the palm of my hand and the G string (fig. 12). Now take a look at the different elbow positions in the two illustrations (figs. 11 and 12). This elbow rotation means that my fingers will arrive on each string at a similar angle, increasing the accuracy of my intonation.

Fig. 13 is a side view of my left hand in position on the D string. Take notice of the arching of my fingers. Can you spot the following?

- Whole step between my first and second fingers
- Half step between my second and third fingers
- Whole step between my third and fourth fingers

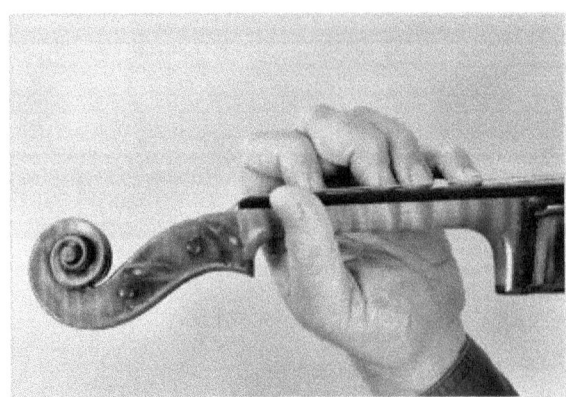

Fig. 13. Thumb and first finger position

Economy of Motion

It's wise to avoid using extra motion and activity when we play. Let's think about our motion "budget" and look at some specific things you can do to avoid overspending the energy stored in your left hand fingers.

A finger will either be in use (pressing the string down against the fingerboard), in position (having been used in a passage and still touching the string), or hovering above the string (awaiting use soon). Be conscious of using only the minimum amount of pressure to depress the playing finger into the string, but also be careful to release that finger when it's not in use, allowing it to remain as relaxed as possible. Keep it close enough to reach the string quickly, in the ready position for the next time it's needed, so it can be ready to move quickly.

Take notice of the distance your fingers keep from the string when they are not in use. Sometimes people flex their unused fingers far away from the fingerboard and this can cause problems, such as not getting back to the string in time, upsetting the rhythm or causing intonation issues. Remember, relaxed fingers pave the way for faster passage work. Use minimum pressure, and keep your fingers down until you need to lift them. This will make it possible for you develop your agility and increase your speed.

Whispering
Melody and Duet

Schonberger
arr. Cohen

Whispering Melody and Duet page 2

Jeremy Cohen with his violin teacher, Itzhak Perlman (left), backstage at Davies Symphony Hall in San Francisco, c. 2001

El Choclo
Rhythmic solidarity

El Choclo (an early tango) achieved international popularity as a crossover hit, and many musicians across multiple styles have penned their own arrangements of it. This treatment is in the swing-jazz style which was popular when the tune first appeared on the musical horizon in the US. *El Choclo* was first performed in Buenos Aires in 1903, it has since surfaced in many forms and styles. A choclo, by the way, is how the Argentines refer to a ear of corn. This piece was written for a club owner, a tough guy whose hair color earned him the nickname "El Choclo."

Notice that *El Choclo* has a clear and concise theme. It has a short and chunky melody with a repeated eighth note rhythmic pattern. Its heavy quarter note beat feel seems strong and relentless, and in fact many tangos have this solid quarter note drive to them. I present it to you here in duet form in the hopes that the two versions—melody as well as improvisation—will encourage rhythmic solidarity between you and your duet partner.

Tango has a 1/4 feeling as opposed to a 4/4 feeling. Achieve this by evenly stressing each beat of the bar. Don't lean on the bar lines, instead play each beat with the sure-footedness of a main beat. Also, pay attention to the dots and dashes. Keep the dotted notes quite short and the dashed notes long and full in order to approach a distinctive tango style.

In the improvisation duet, I chose to make the second voice higher in range than the first voice. In this case you can play either part, but know that the "harmonized" or second part in this song is built above the main voice. This also happens in *21st Century Blues*.

Notice how the backup track gently slows down at the end of the song. We call this a ritard which is an Italian term for slowing down. Make sure your improvisation comes to a graceful finish along with the recorded band track.

El Choclo
Melody and Duet

Angel Villoldo
arr. Cohen

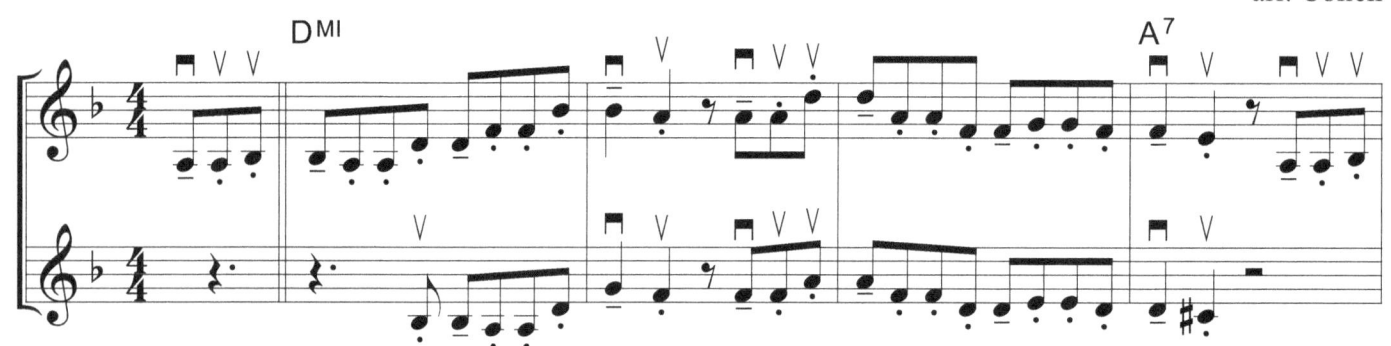

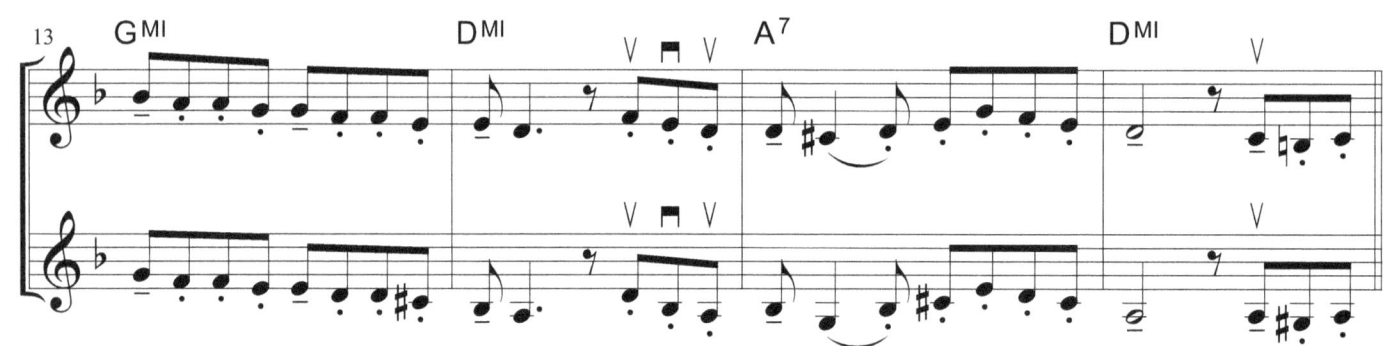

El Choclo Melody and Duet page 2

El Choclo
Improvisation and Duet

Angel Villoldo
arr. Cohen

Copyright © 2018 Violinjazz Publishing (ASCAP)
All rights reserved.
www.violinjazz.com

El Choclo Improvisation and Duet page 2

Jeremy Cohen and Dix Bruce, c. 1988

Jeremy Cohen with jazz pianist, composer and arranger Horace Silver, 1982

Indiana
Right arm and bow coordination

The bowings in *Indiana* will work well if you keep your bow mostly on or close to the string. It might be a difficult piece to sight-read, but with a bit of practice you'll find that it all works well on the instrument. Be patient—it will require some study, but you will be rewarded!

An anticipated beat adds a strong jazzy element to the melody. Look in Bar 1 at the dotted quarter note of beat one, which anticipates or "pushes" the second beat. You'll find similar rhythmic events in Bars 2 and 8, 16 and 18, and a few other spots as well. Work carefully to get your bow arm to articulate these moments with rhythmic clarity. Think about the choreography of your right arm — be ready to play that pushed eight note accurately. If you feel the pushed beats in your right hand wrist and fingers, you'll deliver a truly swinging feel to the Melody.

In the improvisation and duet of Indiana, the two successive downbows (Bar 11) and upbows (Bar 24) might seem tricky the first time through, but they will keep the bow in position at the balance point so you express a swinging rhythm with a confident sound. Starting the bow in the same direction can take a few microseconds, but these bowings are designed to keep us in strict time while delivering a solid swinging style.

Have a look at the quarter rest between Bars 23 and 24 in the improvisation and duet version. Plenty of time exists for a quick pickup of the bow (Bar 23, beat four) and placing it back down on the string for the downbeat (Bar 24, beat one). Practice this a few times, making sure you stay with the time structure. Don't let your arm fall behind the beat—be ready for these double bowings ahead of time. That's what practice is for!

> While most string players carefully try to avoid making mistakes, it's important to try things out. Don't worry if they don't sound successful to your ear on the first or second try. Just keep at it.

Loose fingers and flexible joints on your bow hand are key in playing this arrangement at tempo with the provided backup track. Listen carefully to the audio track in order to understand how it feels to play in a swing ensemble. In the guitar track, the back beat (stresses on beats two and four) serves as a percussion part. Match up the rhythm of your playing with this swinging feel.

Indiana
Melody and Duet

Hanley and MacDonald
arr. Cohen

Copyright © 2018 Violinjazz Publishing (ASCAP)
All rights reserved.
www.violinjazz.com

Indiana Melody and Duet page 2

Indiana Melody and Duet page 3

Indiana
Improvisation and Duet

Hanley and McDonald
arr. Cohen

Indiana Improvisation and Duet page 2

Indiana Improvisation and Duet page 3

Django's Djazz Blues
Transpositions and hooked bowings

You are likely to meet a musician or singer who knows the same song as you, but in a different key. How can you prepare yourself for this moment? By knowing how to play the melody and a solo over chords that may not be the ones you expect! This kind of flexibility is very important for musicians. Our focus here is to learn how to play a melody in multiple keys.

On the play-along band track *Django's Djazz Blues* goes to seven different keys, beginning in the key of G and then modulating up a perfect fourth to the key of C. The modulations continue up by perfect fourths to F, Bb, Eb, Ab, and finally Db. I've written the melody and improvisation in the first two keys, G and C. Once you're comfortable in those keys, try transposing the melody and improvisation to the other keys. Experiment with this—professional jazz musicians need to be ready to transpose and play in any key. It might be difficult at first but with practice it is doable.

We shouldn't limit ourselves to certain keys, convincing ourselves that one key is easier or harder than another. My philosophy here is that the violin is essentially a "keyless" instrument. It is not meant to be easier to play in one key than another. Our worlds are made up of half steps, whole steps, intervals, four open strings, and that's about it! If we understand our half steps, whole steps and intervals, then it's no biggie when the open strings aren't available.

> I believe that things are hard when you tell yourself they are hard. So tell yourself it's not that hard, and work on a way to get it done. You will be happy you did.

Most of the difficulty people perceive about playing in certain keys is simply fear or hesitation. If you understand the relationships of what's happening between your fingers—the half and whole steps—you'll find that the violin is an "equal opportunity" instrument. No single key should be easier to play in than another. Half steps will always be half steps, and the same for whole steps. What we need to understand better is how to apply concepts of shifting and finger placements in all keys.

When learning a new piece, you may have difficulty finding certain pitches because you aren't hearing those pitches in advance (it's a new piece, after all). Try marking your half steps, whole steps, and shifts on the page with a pencil (or stylus, on a screen) so you're ready for the move and can see it as it approaches. Even after all these years of playing, I still find markings useful, but just the ones that I need, nothing extra. I erase or cover the markings I don't need in order to keep my music as neat and clean as possible. Mark only what's needed and avoid clutter on the page.

You'll see some hooked bowings (or bowings across the beats) in many phrases in this piece, in both the melody and the improvisation. Bowing across beats is an interesting way to create a swinging back beat feel in any piece you are playing.

Pay attention to the dashed note at the end of Bar 13 in the improvisation. I lengthened this note to provide some energy towards the sound of the new key. Can you hear how that slightly longer note gives renewed energy to the musical line and an anticipation of the key change? I also put little crescendos on the long notes at the end of Bars 2, 6, 15, and 19, as well as decrescendos in Bars 4, 8, 17 and 21. These are small additions of bow speed and pressure to help propel us from the uphill climb of the line into the downhill motion. Anticipate the musical waves in this improvisation by using crescendos and decrescendos—they will add a whole new level of interest to your playing!

Notice that the backup track modulates into other keys as well. Continue transposing this piece along with the band on the audio track into the new keys. See if you can modulate the melody into the new keys. Experiment with this—professional jazz musicians need to do this type of thing regularly.

Note: The slow audio tracks do not include repeats. When playing along with the recordings play only the second endings.

Jeremy Cohen with jazz educator, pianist, composer Billy Taylor and violinist Roy Malan at the Rockport Opera House in Maine, 2000

Django's Djazz Blues
Melody

Dix Bruce
arr. Cohen

Django's Djazz Blues
Improvisation

Dix Bruce
arr. Cohen

Red Wing Swing

Bow use for long and short notes
Understanding the balance point and weight of the bow

Red Wing Swing is all about leaving the bow down on or at the level of the string. It should be played at the balance point of the bow, almost entirely without the bow ever leaving the string. Most people would guess that the middle of the stick would be the center point of our bows, but it's not. To find the balance point, first locate the spot that is the exact middle point of the stick. Now move a few inches toward the frog. That is where you will find the balance point of the bow. In fig. 13 I'm holding the bow at its balance point, and the white tape shows the bow's middle point.

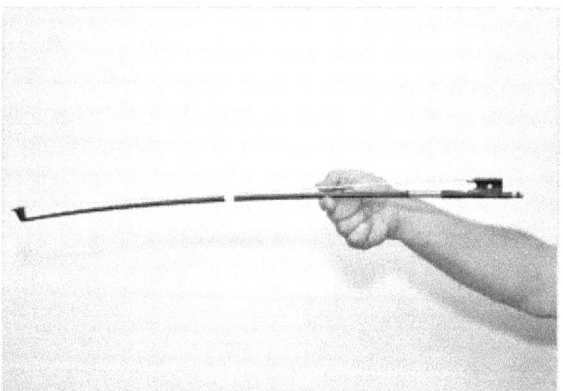

Fig. 13. *Holding the bow at the balance point.* White tape is marking the middle of the bow.

Fig. 14. *Playing at the balance point of the bow.* I am playing beyond or below the center of the stick and a couple of inches closer to the frog. Notice that my right arm shoulder and elbow are fairly low and relaxed.

You can experiment with finding the balance point of your bow by holding out your hand, extending your first finger, and balancing your bow on it. (Be sure to do this over a bed or a soft surface in case you drop your bow!) Find the spot where the bow rests on your finger without teetering in one direction or the other. When you do this, you'll see that the bow balance point is closer to the frog than the middle of the stick. This is where we can simply let the bow rest on the string without adding or subtracting any weight with our fingers or grip.

> Remember this: the contact point between the bow and the string should be at the balance point of the bow.

The natural weight of the bow rests perfectly at this balance point and we don't need to apply any energy up, down, or any other way. A gentle bow hold—using just enough energy to keep things in place—is plenty. How much more energy do you use to keep your bow in place than this? Players typically force way too much energy through their fingers into their bow grip than is actually useful for easy and healthy basic tone production.

> Fun Fact: The violin only weighs about a pound, and the bow only weighs about two ounces!

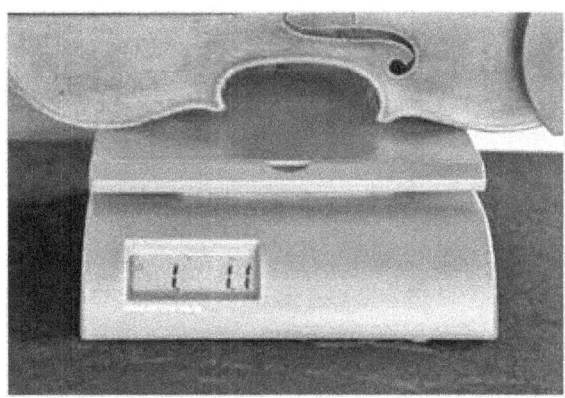

Fig. 15. Postal scale reveal, part 1. My violin comes in at 1 pound, 1.1 ounces.

Fig. 16. Postal scale reveal, part 2. My bow comes in at exactly 2 ounces.

Go ahead and experiment with this. You might be slinging enough tension to actually be holding a five-pound bow, so become very conscious about how much weight and pressure you are applying to your instrument and bow. I encourage you to find an easy and comfortable way to play songs and explore rhythms using this light bow grip. If you do, you'll find that the weight of the stick is evenly distributed, and it only takes a minimum of effort to play comfortably at this location.

Lastly, I'll point out that the right hand fingers and lower arm (forearm, not upper arm) do all the work to bring out the swing rhythms. We want to use our bow like a drummer uses his or her drumstick (although our bow strokes are horizontal and a drummer uses vertical strokes). Be sure to keep your wrist loose and supple for the direction changes from down to up. If your wrist is stiff, the music won't swing. Keep your right shoulder and elbow low and relaxed. Let the bow fingers create the articulations. On the short or dotted notes, make sure the bow comes to a complete stop.

Are you holding your instrument with tension?

The violin weighs only one pound. Think about how tightly you hold on to it with your jaw, head, or left hand, and become aware of how much tension you use to grip your two-ounce bow. Try holding your instrument and bow using the minimum amounts of pressure or force (without dropping them of course). How much energy does it take? Are you using too much in the course of your normal playing? Just enough? Take some time to experiment with this.

Feel the force of gravity when holding up your violin. Let its natural weight drop into your left hand. Now meet that gravitational weight with just enough resistance to keep the instrument suspended, parallel to the floor and in proper place for playing.

Most players tense up to play and then attempt to relax their energy down to get a nice tone. I suggest you try approaching it from the opposite direction, using only enough energy to suspend your left arm without it collapsing back to your side.

Get in touch with feeling the natural pull of gravity gently drawing your arm toward the floor. Hold your arm out in front of you, giving it some resistance, and ask someone to gently push down on your hand. Your arm should teeter gently from your shoulder, springing back to its extended position when the pushing stops. Keep this in mind: your instrument and bow don't weigh much, so you don't need to use much energy to hold them up!

Red Wing Swing
Melody

Kerry Mills
arr. Bruce

Red Wing Swing
Improvisation

Kerry Mills
arr. Cohen

Copyright © 2018 Violinjazz Publishing (ASCAP)
All rights reserved.
www.violinjazz.com

Stumbling
Springy energy in the right hand and arm

I hope the title and lyrics of this piece trigger your imagination and suggest how you might play it.

> Stumbling all around, stumbling all around,
> Stumbling all around so funny,
> Stumbling here and there, stumbling ev'ry-where,
> And I must declare,
> I stepped right on her toes,
> And when she bumped my nose,
> I fell and when I rose, I felt a-shamed and told her,
>
> "That's the latest step, that's the latest step,
> That's the latest step, my honey,
> Notice all the pep, Notice all the pep,
> Notice all the pep."
> She said, "Stop mumbling, though you are stumbling,
> I like it just a little bit, just a little bit,
> Quite a little bit."

Look at the melody in Bars 1 and 2. The short rising lines in a three beat pulse put us off balance with the time signature. We see the same thing happening in Bars 5 and 6 with the descending lines. I took this concept and applied it to the improvisation by using staccato marks and eighth rests. These slight pauses are short hiccups or gaps, and the time value of these spaces are equal to the time values of the notes. In fact, the rests are an important part of the music, as important as the notes.

Remember, when you are playing the lead melodic voice, you are also in charge of the rhythmic feel. The rests are more than just momentary breaks in the sound—they are also functional elements of the musical line.

Now look at the triplets in Bar 4 and 9 of the improvisation and notice how their speed gives the impression of falling forward, or stumbling. You'll also see a number of "downup-up-down" bowings. Take a look at Bars 15 through 17 and Bar 18, where the bowing pattern suggests the idea of gently tripping and falling forward. Reflect this in your bow arm when you play the springy down-up-up motifs. Keep the dotted notes quite short and play the dashed notes with their full value, staying accurate with the metronomic time. By doing this, you will be providing your own rhythm section and communicating security with your style. Leave the bow relaxed and on the string. Use relaxation instead of tension.

I'd be remiss if I didn't say something about how to play those chromatic (or half step) triplets in Bar 9. Be prepared ahead of time with the movement of those left hand fingers on the half steps. Practice carefully and play the triplets absolutely evenly, making sure that the three notes of the triplet add up to the same time value of a single quarter note. Follow them with a snappy short dotted quarter note and you will be speaking the language of swing!

Interpretation: Moving from Classical to Jazz

We are taught that a good sense of rhythm is an important skill, regardless of the style of music we are playing. This is true indeed. But we are asked to go another step when playing jazz and swing. We need to understand that the language of jazz has rhythm in the individual notes and the relationships between them. In jazz, we use a more articulated sound than in classical music because the style requires it. In classical music, solid time is crucial but the quality of the melody carries most of the importance and interest. In jazz, melody and rhythm carry equal weight. Developing rhythmic presence in our melodic lines is necessary for swing.

Stumbling
Melody

Zez Confrey
arr. Cohen

Stumbling
Improvisation

Zez Confrey
arr. Cohen

Jeremy with bass guitarist and Carol Kaye at the Henry Mancini Institute in Los Angeles, c. 2006.

Jeremy with Grammy and Oscar winning composer and arranger Johnny Mandel at the Henry Mancini Institute in Los Angeles, 2006

Tiger Rag

Light and active bow arm and wrist

Tiger Rag is a simple song with brief melodic bits strung together, resulting in a wild ride. Over the years it has become a Dixieland and swing-jazz standard. This tune provides a great opportunity to discover the concept of "less is more."

The melody works best when we don't expel too much downward pressure into the instrument from the bow through our bow stroke. To make a good tone we need to keep our upper and lower arm light and flexible. Let me explain how this works.

When we put the bow down on the string, the downward pressure of the natural weight of the bow causes tension between the bow hair and the string. After you put the bow down on the string, I want you to release that downward pressure as you move your arm horizontally. In that moment when you release the pressure, you'll be creating a tiny accent or articulation, which starts the note with a full tone. Allow the energy of the bow stroke to glide effortlessly across the string, causing the instrument to vibrate freely. Practice each note of the melody slowly, using this technique, and listen for the gentle articulation of each quarter note.

The dashes on the eighth notes in Bars 3 and 4 signal you to keep the bow on the string and keep your right arm active and in motion. Allow your movement and energy to be horizontal rather than vertical and keep the bow close to the balance point so very little effort is necessary to articulate each note.

Starting at Bar 58, the even numbered bars each have a little slide release indication on the end of the second note in the bar. (The marking looks like a little eyelash falling from the note head.) These mini "fall offs" are typical in the jazz idiom. Listen to how I play them on the audio track and notice that they diminish in intensity rather than get stronger. Each one fades away from the note.

The end of Bar 81 includes a slide into the last note of the bar—make sure the slide starts lightly and increases its intensity up to the note following the slide. Now you are articulating like a real jazz player!

When you play the *Tiger Rag* improvisation duet, apply the same technique of staying light with the bow. Doing so will articulate the short notes clearly and keep the style bouncy and light. Each time you see a rest in the duet (e.g. Bars 16–24) practice returning the bow to the string during the rest. Relax the right arm, starting the next note from the string surface rather than dropping the bow from above the string. This kind of clean articulation lends itself to a jazzy style. You can apply this bow control skill to many pieces in the swing jazz repertoire as well as many other genres. Have fun experimenting and adding this technique to your stylistic tool box.

Tiger Rag
Melody

Harry DeCosta, Edwin Edwards,
Nick LaRocca, Tony Spargo,
and Larry Shields

arr. Cohen

Tiger Rag Melody page 2

Tiger Rag
Improvisation and Duet

Harry De Costa, Edwin Edwards,
Nick La Rocca, Tony Spargo,
Larry Shields
arr. Cohen

Copyright © 2018 Violinjazz Publishing (ASCAP)
All rights reserved.
www.violinjazz.com

Tiger Rag Improvisation and Duet page 3

Tiger Rag Improvisation and Duet page 4

Jeremy's Jamboree
Developing your own solos

This piece is built on the chord progression of a song that was an old hit from 100 years ago. Take a look at the melody, and then look at how I crafted the improvisation. You'll see that it is similar, yet different. The melody is simpler to remember or whistle, while the improvisation—though rooted in the melody—departs from the tune in "fiddlistic" ways. Look for some rhythmizing and neighboring tones (the E-flat at the end of the second full bar, and the E-flat to E-natural in the middle of Bar 9). These neighboring notes are winding around while not wandering too far from the melody. I'm retelling the melody with embellishments that feature the following:

- More complex melodic lines, which use half steps
- Energetic rhythms and a more active bow arm
- Quotes of the song's melody with short subtle departures from it

In creating an improvisation I am building a new song on the harmonic progression foundation of the original song. Now take a look at the underlying chords. You can improvise over these harmonies, so try this in your practice:

- Identify the chord that is being played by the band—you'll see these chord names in your score (C, A7, D7, and so on).

- Craft simple patterns based on those chords by simply breaking the chords apart into arpeggios. Simple arpeggiated patterns based on chords are useful for understanding the harmonic structure of a song, and for recognizing different chord progressions from song to song.

Too frequently we focus entirely on the melody line of a song without knowing that all melody lines work well one way or another over a specific chord, because they are answering to that chord, or even working against it in a constructive or creative way.

Go ahead and experiment altering your melody lines or arpeggiating and rhythmizing chords. These are all great tools for greasing the wheels to bring your improvising chops up to speed.

Jeremy's Jamboree
Melody

Jeremy Cohen

Jeremy's Jamboree
Improvisation

Jeremy Cohen

Have Pity

Smooth legato playing and long bow strokes

Have Pity is in 3/4 or "waltz time." The two sections modulate back and forth between minor and major keys. The challenge for us in this smooth, melodic piece is the constant changing between strings in order to play the melody. In Bar 2 the melody requires us to cross two strings. So, in order to keep a smooth line, the bow arm needs to be ready for these moves in advance.

The first note in Bar 2 is a G on the D string, followed by a third beat G on the E string. If your right arm elbow doesn't arrive on the new string at the proper location, you may get a bump in the tone or a bounce of the bow. To prepare ahead of time, place your elbow at the proper level for the D, and then drop it to the E string level. By doing this you'll preserve a smooth, stable tone. Practice getting your right elbow in the correct position smoothly before the note starts. Achieve this by starting with a relaxed shoulder so the arm can rotate smoothly and easily to the proper level.

Keep your right arm in motion throughout the entire song. It doesn't call for a chunky or rhythmic swing style; it needs a more relaxed, flowing, and smooth arm. So keep that right arm expressing horizontal motion and keep it moving. Use the entire length of the bow, from the frog to the tip, allowing the bow to remain light. Avoid pressing into the string with the right hand fingers for sound. Get your tone and volume from increasing your horizontal motion, keeping vertical pressure to a minimum. Remember, the bow only weighs about two ounces.

When you work with the backup track, pay attention to the way it slows down at the end. Be ready for a gentle *ritard* as the song finishes up—your bandmates will appreciate the touch of class you add here as you all come in for a smooth landing together.

Vibrato

Vibrato is a technique, an "additive" to our sound that gives it a specific flavor and style. The Oxford Dictionary of Music tells us this: vibrato is "a slight fluctuation of pitch produced on sustained notes by an oscillating motion of the left hand."

Generally, vibrato cues the listener towards a "classical" sound. Classical players are taught that near constant use of vibrato is advised whenever possible, but this is not necessarily the case for the jazz musician. I personally do choose to use vibrato for color at specific moments in my jazz playing, adding it only where its use gives color, animation, or emotion to an individual note or passage. It's a conscious choice, but not a default setting. Learn to play without it, adding it in for effect from time to time. Many of the jazz greats do use vibrato, but very judiciously.

Vibrato has a variety of types, differentiated by where and how the left arm generates the vibrating. Some players use an upper arm vibrato, while others use a wrist or a finger vibrato. These different techniques deliver vastly different results in sound and style.

I suggest one important thing to keep in mind. Wherever in your body you generate your vibrato, make sure that the highest point of the individual shake or wiggle of the oscillation is on the pitch of the note you're playing. In other words, don't let your vibrato rise above the absolute "in tune" pitch. A healthy vibrato oscillates from the pitch to below the pitch and back up to the pitch—it never goes above the absolute pitch. Here's why: the listener's ear hears the highest part of the vibrato shake as the primary note. If your vibrato rises above this note, your intonation will sound sharp. Test this theory out.

Have Pity
Melody

Traditional
arr. Cohen

Jeremy Cohen's **Make Your Fiddle Swing!**

Have Pity
Improvisation and Duet

Traditional
arr. Cohen

I Ain't Got Nobody
Rhythmizing the melody

I thought it would be a good idea to have a discussion in this book about how to develop a conversation between your inner ear (audiation) and your instrument.

In my mind (and usually in the shower) I am a world famous singer, and you probably are as well. Stadiums full of adoring fans are enjoying our performance as we fearlessly sing our favorite songs. As it turns out, we are lucky to be string players because our instruments provide the vehicle for our voice—our instruments *are* our voices. The thing I want us to think about here is how make sure that our singer voice, that voice inside our head, is channeled efficiently through our instruments. If you play and also sing in your group then you are a multi-instrumentalist, and bravo to you!

Even though we are playing an instrument, in a sense we are doing exactly what singers do—we are interpreting a song by adding color, rhythm, and style with our bow arms, with our left hand fingers, combining them all to create our unique voice. We have the responsibility to sing through our instruments. This involves giving dynamics, shapes, and rhythms to the melodies and improvisations we play.

Let's dig a little deeper into this through *I Ain't Got Nobody*, which demonstrates numerous ways of interpreting notes within a song by adding mixed rhythms, without altering the sequence of the melody. I call this "rhythmizing."

The long notes in this melody have been broken up into rhythmic bits, or subdivisions, to create a rhythmized version of the melody by giving it a swinging rhythm. This allows me to become both a melodic and rhythmic contributor to the band. Compare the melody with the improvisation and you'll find the same notes played in different rhythms. Rhythmizing a melody can be a useful tool in developing your own personal style—it's similar to adding spices to a meal to make it more interesting. You will also make yourself more useful to an ensemble if you can add rhythm elements and be a supportive voice when it's time for other members to be featured.

I Ain't Got Nobody
Melody

Spencer Williams
arr. Cohen

I Ain't Got Nobody
Rhythmized Melody

Spencer Williams
arr. Cohen

Rhythmization

When I "rhythmize," I change the rhythm of the melody without changing the pitches of the melody.

To play a swing style rhythm, start with two eighth notes. Instead of playing them equal in length, try playing them as the first and third notes of a triplet, imagining that the second note of the triplet is tied to the first resulting in a long-short rhythmic pattern.

We can also rhythmize by breaking down a long note into smaller divisions and adding an accent: turn a half note into two eighth notes plus an accented quarter note, for example.

Mixing up the rhythm (in a good way!) can be done to just about any melody. Go to YouTube and listen to the same song interpreted by several different artists. Each artist expresses the same melody in a unique way by applying different accents, articulations, and emphases, and you may enjoy one more than another. Listening to multiple versions of the same song is a great way to expand your own rhythmization skills.

Trying to understand and recreate these differences while adding your own ideas will help you develop your own personal style and sound.

Jeremy with pianist-composer Dave Brubeck at Mills College, Oakland, CA, 2005. Brubeck is holding Jeremy's string quartet arrangement of one of Brubeck's greatest hits, "Blue Rondo a la Turk," following Jeremy's performance of the piece with Quartet San Francisco at a concert dedicated to Brubeck's music

Way Down Yonder in New Orleans
Expressing solid time

I enjoy the melody of *Way Down Yonder In New Orleans* and here are a few reasons why: I like the way the opening phrase starts on the beat, and the second phrase (Bar 3) starts off the beat. I also like that this melody has a definite four-bar phrase that functions as a call and response—the first two bars behave like a question, and the second two bars behave like an answer. This tune has an upbeat and positive feeling to it, and it makes me wish I could visit New Orleans immediately. I miss it so.

Pay attention to the clean stops in Bars 13 and 17. They help us differentiate the first twelve bars from the second twelve bars of the melody by lending a new and wonderful bit of musical information. Treat that passage differently than you would the opening bars of the piece.

Be careful to use economy of motion in Bar 16 of the improvisation. In other words slow down your bow speed, stay in the lower half of the bow in order to retake the bow back to the frog (or lower half of the bow) for the chord on beat 4. Otherwise you may find yourself too far out towards the tip of the bow to get to the chord in solid metronomic time, causing you to fall behind the band.

One of the common factors we all share as string players is the fact that we use a bow which basically travels in two directions. As we travel the distance of the bow from the frog to the tip, we find our right hand increasingly farther away from our instrument. I compare it to having a drumstick that gets longer and longer, distancing our hand (our source of articulation) from the string. This distance can affect the timing and rhythm of our articulations.

Because of the back and forth motion of the bow arm, we occasionally find ourselves lagging behind the beat of the band, losing rhythmic drive. Practicing for this ahead of time helps us stick with the swinging rhythms, lending a fluency to our jazz language, regardless of the location of our point of contact between the bow and the string. Listen carefully and don't fall behind the beat or the band.

I heartily encourage developing bow arm techniques to facilitate playing in the middle or lower half of the bow, which keeps us more aligned to metronomic rhythm necessary for playing in jazz idioms. Frequently the rhythm section (guitar, piano, bass, and drums) keeps these rhythms for us, and all we need to do is follow. But a more developed playing concept and bow arm gives us a more complete package: we're not only soloists, we're also full members of the rhythm section, expressing solid time in our melodies and improvisations. It's swing time all the time!

Way Down Yonder in New Orleans
Melody

Creamer & Leighton
arr. Cohen

Way Down Yonder in New Orleans
Improvisation and Duet

Creamer and Layton
arr. Cohen

Copyright © 2018 Violinjazz Publishing (ASCAP)
All rights reserved.
www.violinjazz.com

Way Down Yonder in New Orleans Improvisation and Duet page 2

Wrapping Things Up

I hope you have enjoyed working through "Make Your Fiddle Swing" and that it has given you a better understanding of the process and practice of swing and jazz on the violin. I also hope it has inspired you to examine your playing technique, whatever your chosen instrument may be, with the goal of improving your tone, playing skills, and stylistic voice.

A musician's journey involves listening to yourself critically and reaching deep inside to improve the way you express yourself with increased clarity, accuracy and intention. It is a journey and does not happen instantaneously. With careful work and patience it will improve slowly over time. Progress will happen much faster when you forge a constructive path forward. Aways look for that path to improvement and avoid focusing on the negative aspects of your playing.

The rewards will be many, and remember, the more you learn, the more you'll find there is to learn. That realization can be overwhelming but it is a critical part of embracing the learning process. Take it a step at a time and you'll keep on learning.

I look forward to hearing your comments or questions regarding this book or any of my other publications. To send comments or questions, or to join our email list for info about new publications and performances, send a message to **information@violinjazz.com**. I hope to continue to stay in touch with you via masterclasses, workshops, and online teaching and videos.

Here's hoping that expressing yourself through music brings ever greater pleasure to you and those who enjoy listening to your music. Keep up the good work!

Jeremy Cohen
Fall 2018

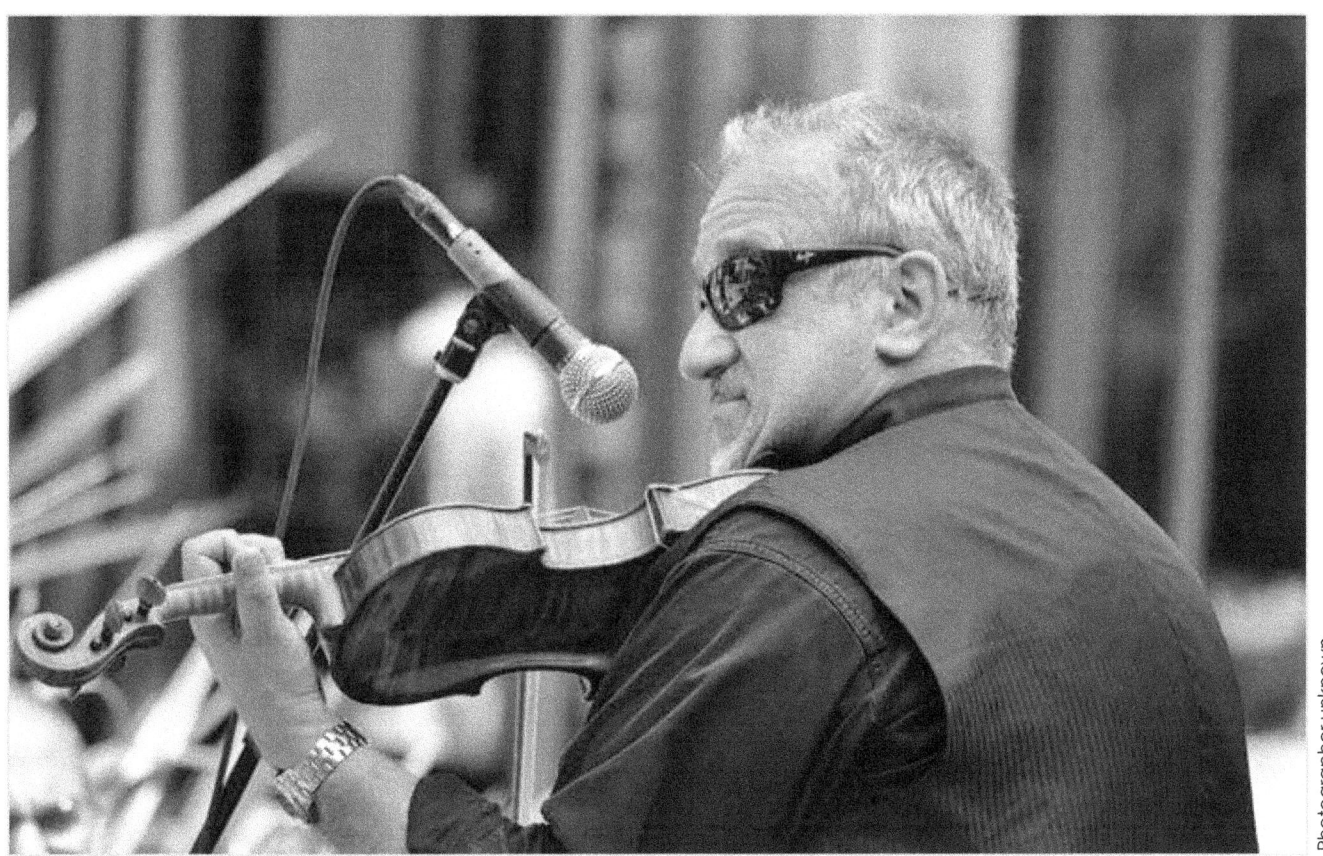

Jeremy Cohen performing in San Francisco, 2015

More by Jeremy Cohen

BOOKS AND SHEET MUSIC AVAILABLE AT VIOLINJAZZ.COM

Stylistic Etudes for Solo Violin
Stylistic Duets for Two Violins
Stylistic Duets for Two Violas
Stylistic Duets for Violin and Cello
Swing Jazz with Hot Club Rhythm
(book and audio set)

Some of These Days / St. Louis Blues
(swing-jazz classics for string quartet)

Comme Il Faut / Francini
(tangos for string quartet)

World Chamber Series for String Quartet
(sold together or separately)

- How Sweet the Sound
- Jasmine Flower
- Jesusita Polka
- Jambo
- Mexican Hat Dance

The Latin Collection
(string quartet pieces, sold together or separately)

- Crowdambo (mambo)
- El dia que me quieras (tango)
- Tango Toscana (quintet with bass and strings, orchestra versions available)
- Tanguori (tango)

Dave Brubeck Collection
(string quartet arrangements of works by jazz pianist Brubeck, sold together or separately)

- Blue Rondo a la Turk
  (quintet version with bass also available)
- Strange Meadowlark

Raymond Scott Collection
(string quartet arrangements of Scott's character pieces, sold together or separately)

- The Penguin
- Powerhouse, arr. by Larry Dunlap
- Siberian Sleighride
- Toy Trumpet

RECORDINGS

Jeremy Cohen: Violinjazz CDs
The Music of Eddie South (Dorian 2010)
A Taste of Violin Jazz (Violinjazz 2010)
Violin Jazz (Violinjazz 2010)

Jeremy Cohen: Quartet San Francisco CDs
A QSF Journey (Reference 2018)
Pacific Premieres: New Works by California Composers (Violinjazz 2013)
QSF Plays Brubeck (Violinjazz 2009)
Whirled Chamber Music (Violinjazz 2007)
Latigo (Violinjazz 2006)

Digital downloads available from violinjazzpublishing.com

www.ingramcontent.com/pod-product-compliance
Lightning Source LLC
Chambersburg PA
CBHW080553170426
43195CB00016B/2771